Original title:
The Final Chapter

Author: Patrick Smith
ISBN HARDBACK: 978-9908-0-0264-4
ISBN PAPERBACK: 978-9908-0-0265-1

An Outstretched Hand

In a world of all things wild,
A hand pops up, a little child.
"Can you help me?" they call with glee,
As I trip on air, oh woe is me!

With toys in pockets, I can't escape,
Here comes a dog—oh no, it's a scrape!
My outstretched hand, it finds no cease,
Just a muddy paw, so much for peace!

Journeys Drawn to a Close

Riding trains that never halt,
Lost a ticket? That's my fault!
With laughter echoing through the air,
I wave goodbye to my last hair!

As buses come and buses go,
I can't recall which way to flow.
But with a grin, I see the light,
And that's enough to feel just right!

The Final Brushstroke

With canvas bare, I splatter paint,
At last it's done? I'm not sure... wait!
A swirl of colors, what a mix,
Is this my masterpiece or silly tricks?

The brush in hand, I shake and dread,
A drop of red lands on my head!
But art is messy, that's my claim,
A rogue Picasso, yes, that's my game!

Reflections at Dusk

As twilight creeps, I check my hair,
But where's the mirror? It's not fair!
I peer at shadows, what a sight,
A funky dance—oh, what a fright!

I ponder life, am I just a fool?
Chasing ducks by the local pool.
With all these thoughts, I chuckle loud,
Reflections dim—but I'm so proud!

Fading Ink

My pen ran dry, what a plight,
Characters vanished into the night.
Pages crinkle, my story's frail,
Is it too late for a martini and ale?

Got plot twists tangled in my hair,
Tripped on a pun, did I dare?
Just when I thought I'd hit the chord,
I realized my punchline's been ignored!

Beyond the Last Verse

With rhymes so silly, I've danced all day,
Forgot my lines, what can I say?
The audience chuckles, they roll their eyes,
Maybe it's time to win the prize!

The lights dim low, here comes the end,
Was that a script or a sketch my friend?
Take a bow, then slip on a shoe,
Oops! Is that laughter I hear? Oh, boo!

The Curtain Falls

The curtain’s dropping, oh what a show,
Did I forget who I'm meant to know?
Silly antics in a dramatic flair,
A flock of ducks, and not a single bear!

The applause is loud, but my mind's a mess,
Did I even wear pants? Time to confess!
Bowing in style, I trip on a friend,
Guess this goodbye is on the mend!

Muffled Goodbyes

Caught in whispers, what did they say?
"Is that a plot twist, or just cliché?"
Muffled giggles amid the confusion,
At least my blunders spark some illusion!

Leaving the stage, I wave and grin,
Is this the exit, or just a spin?
With each step back, the laughter grows,
Maybe my scripts could use more puns, who knows?

Silent Soliloquy

I once had a cat, quite chatty,
Who thought he could sing a ballad.
He howled at the moon,
While my neighbors just stood there, salad.

His meows were a mix, a true symphony,
In the realm of the confused and absurd.
I pondered my patience,
As he struck every note unheard.

Yet each serenade brought me delight,
Even when off-key and wrong.
And in the end, I just laughed,
At my musical feline’s throng.

A Journey's End

At last, I arrive at this cafe,
Where pastries are piled like a tower.
I spent all my cash on a muffin,
With enough icing to make it a flower.

I took a big bite, then a second,
But forgot I had not cleared my plate.
In a rush to devour dessert,
I sent my fork on a wild state!

Cake flew like confetti, a sugar parade,
While the barista just laughed at my plight.
I waved like a clown, crumbs on my face,
This journey's end, simply sweet and light.

Threads of Memory

In the attic, old boxes did wait,
Filled with knickknacks from years past.
I found a sock, cozy and warm,
And wondered how long it would last.

Pictures of friends, with hair that defies,
Fashion faux pas from decades ago.
They smiled and waved, my stylish crew,
Thinking their outfits were quite the show.

A toy robot sputtered, in need of repair,
I chuckled at memories, happy and bright.
For even the odd, can spark enough joy,
In the threads of life's colorful light.

Lasting Impressions

A grand finale wrapped in sparkles,
With party hats and silly cheers.
I slipped on a pie, oh what a sight,
The laughter rang for days, it appears!

To the clowns, I waved, with jelly on cheeks,
Their honks matched my rhythmic falls.
As they juggled my dreams, along with my hopes,
Who knew that life could be such a ball?

So here's to the mess, the hiccups we face,
For each fumble adds to our show.
In the end, we find joy in mischief,
Where the brightest memories glow.

Epilogue of Echoes

Once upon a time, it seems,
A hero lost his flair for dreams.
He tripped on words, fell on his face,
While chasing plot in a frantic race.

The villain laughed and rolled his eyes,
As chapters flew like paper flies.
With every twist, the script was bent,
A comedy gold, a laugh was sent.

The sidekick stood with popcorn near,
To witness mayhem, joy, and cheer.
In twisted tales of epic blunders,
Laughter echoed through countless wonders.

So cheers to tales that go askew,
With every turn, a laugh that's due.
For when the ink begins to dry,
A giggle lingers, oh my, oh my!

Last Verses in Twilight

As daylight fades and shadows bide,
The plot thickens with wit and pride.
Characters munch on popcorn fate,
While the book waits, oh can’t be late!

With each new line, the laughter flows,
A hero? No, it's just a pose.
He’s tripping over his silly feet,
A clumsy tale, oh isn’t it sweet?

The clock ticks down, but here comes fate,
A twist that’s sure to resonate.
As whispers rise and giggles soar,
We ponder if there’s more in store.

So raise a glass to playful prose,
As twilight wraps and laughter grows.
For in this tale of blunders rife,
We find the joy, the funny life!

When Pages Turn to Silence

The pages flutter, a gentle sigh,
As characters bid their last goodbye.
The hero trips, spills lemonade,
A final act in this charade.

With laughter loud, the crowd erupts,
As logic bends and chaos erupts.
A villain sneezes, the plot then flips,
A comedic end, no need for scripts.

The quirky sidekick cracks a joke,
While scenes dissolve like morning smoke.
In silent moments, chuckles bloom,
As laughter dances through the room.

So as we close this book so fine,
We find the humor, a silver line.
For when the last words softly glide,
The echoes linger, humor's pride!

Shadows of Yesterday

In shadows cast by stories spun,
The laughter echoes, one by one.
Once heroes fought and villains sneered,\nNow just a joke, how we’ve cheered!

The ghost of stories, silly winks,
As characters embrace their shrinks.
With every twist, a tumble here,
For laughter reigns, let’s give a cheer!

The ending’s near, but not quite done,
These pages held mischief and fun.
Beneath their laughs, a wink remains,
A memory wrapped in comic chains.

So close the book with a hearty laugh,
Recall the gaffes on this wild path.
For in the shadows where tales get shy,
A giggle blooms, oh me, oh my!

Eclipsed by Memory

In a library filled with dust,
The tales we told turned to rust.
Characters dance on the shelf,
Tripping over their own self.

Forgotten plots start to snore,
As I search for that one scene once more.
But even the bookmarks look lost,
Reminding me of the high cost.

I laughed at the twists, oh so wild,
Now I’m just a forgetful child.
Plot holes like cheese, full of holes,
More confusing than your average trolls.

The ending’s a riddle, a jumbled mess,
Like trying to dress in a giant dress.
Still, I chuckle at the unfinished fight,
As the book closes gently, goodnight!

A Story's Gentle Fade

Once the pages were crisp and bright,
Now the ink is escaping from sight.
Heroes once bold now wear reading glasses,
While villains just sit, waiting for passes.

The plot began with a wild chase,
Now we walk at a leisurely pace.
A twist turns to fumble, a slip and a slide,
Once we were gallant, now we just hide.

Ending scenes swap seats with dull chatter,
While I search for the crux of the matter.
Time flies like a pie in the air,
Oops! Is that pudding? Remember to share!

Yet laughter remains, our bittersweet note,
Narratives drift on a whimsical boat.
As the story fades softly into the blue,
I wonder what happened to you!

In the Shadow of Twilight

As the sun dips low beneath the hills,
I ponder where lost laughter spills.
Plot twists that used to shine bright,
Now dance like shadows in twilight.

Once was a quest for the heart's great treasure,
Now it's a nap, finding TV pleasure.
Characters bicker in endless reprise,
Life’s more thrilling with snacks and some fries!

Chasing memories like they’re balloons,
But they've popped, and they left some tunes.
Adventures on pages turn into grass,
Waiting for laughter from each little pass.

Yet here we are, sipping sweet tea,
A story’s soft end, and it’s still carefree.
So let’s chuckle at what’s come to be,
Savor the silliness, just you and me!

The Quiet Ending

The clock strikes slow, as if in a dream,
Once we laughed loud, now we just gleam.
Whispers retreat into cozy nooks,
Happy endings, like rare storybooks.

Where did the heroes dash off in fright?
Perhaps they danced under the moonlight.
Chasing endings that loop in a jar,
Each twist adds humor, like an old guitar.

The laughter fades in a gentle sway,
Characters linger, decide to delay.
Life's not a race, but a cozy chair,
With dust bunnies that wiggle everywhere.

So let's tiptoe into that last line,
With a chuckle that feels so divine.
For even as stories come to a rest,
We still know laughter is simply the best!

The Echo of Solitude

In a room all alone, my socks start to dance,
The cat gives me looks, like it's watching a chance.
Dust bunnies spin tales of their grand, ancient lore,
As I contemplate snacks and procrastinate more.

The fridge hums a tune, it’s quite like a song,
It knows all my secrets, where I truly belong.
With each crumpled bag, a snack’s silent plea,
To savor my solitude, just it and me!

Boredom plays tricks, like a prankster at play,
The goldfish swims circles, it's judging my day.
I laugh at the mirror, it laughs back, what a sight,
Together we jest at this dance of delight!

So here in my realm of whimsical cheer,
I toast to the chaos that brought me right here.
With snacks in my lap and a grin ear to ear,
I embrace the odd moments that bring me good cheer!

An Ending to Remember

The plot thickens nicely, like gravy on fries,
As characters bicker and fame slowly dies.
The hero trips over his own shoe lace tie,
While the villain just laughs and lets out a sigh.

With a twist that's quite goofy, the tale takes a spin,
The sidekick in slippers just lost track of where to begin.
A chase turns to tango near the vegetable stand,
And laughter erupts at this slapstick demand.

The clock ticks with panic, the ink starts to blur,
While the lovers make faces, and awkwardly stir.
The page must be turned, but wait, where's the pen?
"Can someone just help me? I'm lost once again!"

And so as it ends, the laughter confounds,
Though tears may be shed, joy still surrounds.
In memory's embrace, we'll live it once more,
As we pen down the comical tales we adore!

When Pages Scatter

The book lays abandoned, its cover’s askew,
With plot lines in disarray, like my morning shampoo.
Dust motes are dancing, they know it’s all done,
As I flip through the pages, where’s all the fun?

A character trips, and the pen makes a splash,
Words tumble like confetti in this wild, crazy crash.
The ending was close, but then came a freeze,
As my coffee goes cold, oh why, oh why tease?

The hero's fine steed has a mind of its own,
It gallops through dreams while I sit here alone.
The villain is tangled in his mustache of fate,
While laughter erupts at their sudden debate.

So here’s to the moments when pages take flight,
To the stories that fumble but still feel so right.
With giggles and grumbles, let’s raise up a cheer,
For every odd chapter that brings us good cheer!

Final Reflections

In a book where plot just twists,
Every villain has a list.
Characters slippin', flippin' by,
And I dare not ask them why.

Plot holes big as outer space,
Chasing each and every trace.
But wait, there's coffee in between,
Fiction's never truly seen.

I check my watch, it's half past five,
The hero's lost, but still alive.
With every page, the laughter flows,
As strange as last year's fashion shows.

So here's to stories, bold and bright,
Where endings rarely end in fright.
Last words spoken, book now closed,
Guess it's time to seek more prose.

A Book Left Behind

I left my book upon the shelf,
It seems to talk just like myself.
The characters, quite full of sass,
Think they can now surpass my class.

A plot twist found in chapter six,
The bunny jumped, that's just a fix.
I swear it waved goodbye to me,
That sneaky novel with a spree!

In margins, laughter fills the space,
A doodle of a smiling face.
Left behind, it starts to roam,
In search of words, a second home.

But what if books could really flee?
To take a trip, oh, let it be!
I'll join my story, pack a snack,
Together we can plan our whack!

When Time Stopped Turning

The clock ran out when last it chimed,
A scene so wacky, absurdly rhymed.
The characters just danced in place,
While I was stuck with spilled hot grace.

A knight, a dragon, all in line,
Waited for a cup of wine.
But time just giggled, flipped the page,
As if to say, “Let's all engage!”

The villain sneezed, 'twas quite a fright,
The hero laughed, “You've lost this fight!”
When time stood still—what a fine jest,
Chasing moments, these are the best.

We threw confetti, made a scene,
In chapters where we're all quite keen.
So let’s just pause and share a grin,
For every laugh, we surely win!

The Heart's Unraveling

A heart that beats in odd directions,
With comic twists of pure perfection.
In this romance, things get askew,
Like socks without a matching crew.

A love note written in crayon,
While fuzzy squirrels plot their big con.
The date was set; I showed up late,
With waffles stacked upon my plate.

The candle's flame just laughed aloud,
"Hey, here's your date, go be proud!"
But love is chaos, don't you see?
With every word, we lose the key.

So here's to hearts that twist and twirl,
In stories where we swing and swirl.
With every chapter, oh so free,
Let's laugh together, you and me!

Twilight's Embrace

As twilight falls, we search for snacks,
A final feast before the worries relax.
The cat joins in, his whiskers a-fluff,
He claims the last bite, oh that's just tough!

With laughter echoing, we toast with glee,
To moments that mattered, just you and me.
The lanterns flicker, a dance in the dark,
Let's not discuss those moments that spark!

A sudden sneeze leads to chaos around,
Spilled soda rockets all over the ground.
But here's to the mess—the laughter won't cease,
In our twilight embrace, we find our peace!

As stars start to twinkle, we take a deep breath,
A clumsy farewell, but we'll skip the death.
Let's end on a high note, with giggles and cheer,
For this isn't goodbye, it's just rest for a year!

The Last Song Sung

We gather 'round for the final refrain,
With off-key notes that dance like the rain.
The microphone's broken, but who gives a hoot?
Let's belt out our laughter, that's quite the pursuit!

Each verse we create is a tumble and fall,
As grandma insists we give it our all.
The dog starts howling, a backup in play,
This concert's a mess, but we'll sing anyway!

The lyrics are jumbled, a comedic show,
But who's keeping score? Just let it all flow.
We sway with abandon, like leaves in the breeze,
Our finale's absurd, but we do it with ease!

So here's to the giggles, the tunes off the beat,
In this raucous retreat, we stand on our feet.
With laughter our anthem, we opt for the fun,
For even the last song is better with puns!

Unfolding to Silence

As pages turn softly, what's left to unveil?
A cat naps nearby, not reading the tale.
The plot thickens slowly, then suddenly halts,
"More coffee?" we ask, as the tension defaults.

Characters grumble, their futures unsure,
One forgets his name, but he's kind of a bore.
A twist in the plot, but it's lost in the brew,
"Let's just skip to dessert!" we all shout anew!

As silence unravels what's left to be read,
We contemplate snacks, and the warmth of our bed.
So here comes the laughter, let's not shed a tear,
For read aloud moments are ripe for good cheer!

With giggles a-plenty, we close the old tome,
Making room for more stories, right here in our dome.
Though chapters may fade, friendships will stay,
In this unfolding silence, we'll find our own way!

Forgotten Chapters

In dust-covered books, we unearth the past,
Forgotten chapters should have never been cast.
With plot holes and fluff, we laugh at the text,
Did someone really think this was next?

The hero stumbles, slips on a pie,
"Is that a battle cry or dessert?" we cry.
Sidekicks equipped with inflatable swords,
They bumble and stumble, their moves so absurd!

Each turn of the page brings a giggle or two,
With characters flailing, and meandering views.
Plot twists that vanish like socks in a wash,
We chuckle in glee, as the storyline's squashed!

So here's to the stories that never made sense,
With hiccups and blunders that feel so immense.
A toast to the funny, the quirks that we see,
For forgotten chapters are the best recipe!

Endpoints of Existence

When life hands you a plot twist,
Just grab a snack and insist.
Dance like no one’s in the room,
Even if it leads to doom.

Life’s quite a silly ride,
With laughter on the side.
Ghosts wave from the beyond,
Shouting, "Hey! We’re still fond!"

Each misstep we do embrace,
Turns into a comical race.
The finale's just a show,
But we’re stealing the glow!

So lift your glass, take heed!
Let laughter be your creed.
No one really takes the fall,
It’s just a wacky ball!

The Last Goodbye

In pajamas, we proclaim,
No one’s really to blame.
With hugs and quirky grins,
Life's just where the fun begins!

Cakes and candles, all misdeeds,
We sow our funny seeds.
Raise your drink, don't be shy,
We might just start to fly!

Remember all the silly fights,
Like who stole the last bites.
Writing notes in messy scribbles,
Giggles drown our stubborn quibbles!

Final words like comic strips,
Blown dry from laughing tips.
We’ll slip out with a cheer,
Leaving laughter, not a tear!

Hushed Revelations

Secrets whisper in the night,
Muffled laughs take to flight.
Under stars, we giggle low,
Guessing truths in a funny show.

A cat wearing a top hat,
Is this life? Nope, a spat!
Every secret planted here,
Unfolds with a hearty cheer!

Peeking through life's little doors,
Finding jesters on all fours.
With every plot that we compose,
Let’s not take off our funny clothes!

So with whispers and a wink,
Let's push the limits, don't you think?
In the end, we’ll laugh and comply,
As the curtain falls, we’ll fly high!

Echoes of a Story

Once upon a time, they say,
Life was but a grand ballet.
With twirls and slips along the way,
We giggled through the disarray!

In a world where pranks collide,
Joy and jest we cannot hide.
Each chapter ends with something odd,
A sock on fire? Oh my god!

From the pages, laughter spills,
We seek the thrill, embrace the chills.
Writing tales that twist and turn,
With every laugh, a lesson learned!

So turn the page, but don't be late,
For the fun we cultivate.
With echoes ringing in the air,
We'll tell our tales without a care!

The Curtain Falls on Dreams

The stage is set, the lights go dim,
A frog jumps in, the plot's gone grim.
The lead forgot her lines at last,
As audience members begin to blast.

The props are tangled, what a sight,
A sheep just bleated, took flight!
The actors laugh, the scene's a flop,
Is this how we end? Oh, please, just stop!

The usher snores, the popcorn’s gone,
They’ve lost their rhythm, where's the dawn?
A cat walks by, steals the show,
As laughter erupts, a real-life throw!

So here's to dreams that never land,
With wobbly chairs and a wild band.
When curtains fall with such great flair,
We all just smile, we simply care.

Unwritten Endings

A book lies closed, dust on the spine,
Page corners curled, and it looks devine.
The plot’s a mystery, what could it be?
A hero with slippers and tea, oh me!

The characters dance, with socks askew,
While villains trip on the stage they flew.
An owl sings jazz, the dog's in a funk,
And the mouse just told jokes, what a junk!

Authors scribble, but ink ran dry,
They've written a mess, oh me, oh my!
A pun on the last page might just fit,
But the cat has claimed it, let's throw a fit!

So here's to stories that never close,
With jesters and giggles and words in rows.
In a world of ink and jumbled thoughts,
Unwritten endings will tie us in knots!

Closure in the Moonlight

The moonlight twinkles, bids goodnight,
The stars start dancing, what a sight!
A raccoon's pondering under the tree,
Is this the end? Or just a spree?

With sandwiches flying and crumbs galore,
The picnic's a hit, but oh! There's more.
A squirrel's on stage, trying to sing,
But all he does is throw nuts—a fling!

The crickets are buzzing a breakbeat sound,
As fireflies shuffle on the ground.
Who knew closure could be this much fun?
Under the moon, we all come undone.

So here we laugh at the night's sweet end,
With raucous joy, our hearts they mend.
In moonlit moments of pure delight,
We find our closure, and the world feels right!

Reflections of a Fading Story

In the mirror hangs a story told,
Faded pages, but still so bold.
The hero's now a bumbling fool,
With shorts on backward—now that's the rule!

The villain's snoozing, forgot his plan,
While sidekicks bake, the whole thing's a jam.
A mystery wrapped in a slice of pie,
Will they escape? Oh my, oh my!

The climax comes, but oops, they tripped,
The audience gasps, oh how they've flipped!
In tangled tales and silly lore,
We find our laughter—who could ask for more?

So let's raise a toast to stories past,
Where echoes of joy are sure to last.
With every giggle and tale retold,
We craft our endings, both bright and bold!

The Silence After the Storm

The rain has stopped, oh what a sight,
The dog is soggy, and it took a bite.
Umbrellas flipped, like a comedy show,
We laugh at our hair, like it's part of the glow.

Puddles reflect all the laughter and fun,
While neighbors debate, 'Was that lightning or sun?'
Cats on the fence are glaring with glee,
As we slip and slide like we're stuck on TV.

We dance around puddles, with vigor and zeal,
With socks rolling down, it's a surreal deal.
"Watch out!" someone yells, "You'll slip on that tray!"
And we all go tumbling, what a wild play!

So here's to the storm, with its thunderous roar,
It brought us together, oh what a score!
The silence is golden, but laughter's the norm,
In the wreckage of chaos, we find our own form.

The Final Curtain's Embrace

The actor stumbles, trip and a fall,
It's all in the script, or so one would call.
But the audience chuckles, louder each time,
While they wonder if this is a joke or a crime.

The curtain starts drooping, a slow-motion wave,
We're left hanging on, will it sink or be brave?
The lights flicker twice, with drama and flair,
A cat might just wander right in from somewhere!

"Bravo!" shouts one, while another spills drink,
The mood shifts from laughter to just let me think.
But the show must go on, with mishaps galore,
We're now in a scene that we can't help but adore!

As the curtain finally drops, and the cheers erupt,
We'll remember the moments, the spirit corrupt.
With bows and salutes, we leave with a grin,
Here's to the madness; it's where we begin!

Pages Blown by the Winds of Fate

A book on the table is battered and worn,
Its pages are flapping, feeling forlorn.
The breeze is a rascal, it's riding so high,
Turning chapters like moments, oh me, oh my!

The hero just tripped on a plot twist so sweet,
Fell into a puddle, oh what a feat!
Villains now giggle, conspiracies stirred,
While readers are gasping at every absurd word.

A cat leaps in, leaves paw prints on dreams,
The characters bicker, or so it seems.
"Can I have my hat back?" a prince does demand,
While the goose starts to honk, lending chaos a hand!

But with winds of mischief, they dance and they play,
Turning the pages, come what may.
For in every flip, we find laughter and cheer,
Embracing the madness, we hold it so dear.

The Last Scene Unfolds

The curtains all rustle, the lights go dim,
The actors all fumble, and that's on a whim.
The king trips on his cape, it's a sight to behold,
As laughter erupts, and chaos unfolds.

The stagehands are giggling, they're losing their cool,
While the director's fuming, "This isn't the rule!"
But a wink and a smile turn frowns into grins,
As the audience cheers for the hilarity spins.

The plot's gone awry, but who really cares?
The storyline's tangled like old, frizzy hairs.
They dance to their hearts, in a playful display,
As we clutch our sides, laughing all the way.

With bows and confetti and laughter so bright,
The curtain will drop, marking the end of the night.
But we'll leave with a chuckle, a memory to mold,
In the joy of the moment, pure comedy gold.

Pages of Remembrance

As I close this book, what a ride it's been,
With wacky plots and tales of sin.
Characters tripped, oh what a sight,
There's even a cat that took flight!

Now I search for the pages, pages so rare,
Didn't think I'd miss that old chair.
It creaked like a whale, or was it a moose?
But hey, it got me through some great juice!

Did I leave the oven on? Oh, woe is me,
Suddenly this life feels like a comedy!
I'll take the laughs, set the drama aside,
In the end, we just want a fun ride!

So here's to the tales both silly and grand,
Life's a joke, just try to understand.
With every goodbye, there's laughter and cheer,
So let's raise a glass to the end of the year!

The Quiet Farewell

A whisper settled where laughter once bloomed,
Like socks in a dryer, hopes slightly doomed.
The curtain’s falling, but let’s not despair,
At least I’m not wearing those matching brown pairs!

With each awkward wave, my palms start to sweat,
Is this goodbye, or just a big bet?
I joke with the fridge, which is oh-so-still,
It’s got ice cream, and I’ve lost my will!

With clumsy joy, I dance out the door,
Tripped on the mat—oh, but what’s one more?
I’ll miss the chaos, the fun little fights,
Like arguing with the vacuum on quiet nights!

So cheers to the memories, what a grand show,
Filled with giggles and maybe a toe.
Don't shed a tear, just crack a big grin,
For every end, a new tale will begin!

Time’s Final Echo

Tick-tock, my clock said it’s time to go,
With a sandwich in hand and a joke for the show.
Did I leave my laundry? Oh scratch that thought,
The echo of laughter is all that I sought!

Time slipped away like butter on toast,
But honestly, I just miss a good roast.
I’ll reminisce fondly, not with a frown,
At least I’m not stuck in this cheesy town!

The moments we had were simply divine,
Like sipping on punch spiked with a sign.
I may not be perfect, or even the best,
But I promise you fun was my ultimate quest!

So here’s my farewell, with a wink and a snort,
May you keep the laughter in every retort.
For what is a story without a chuckle or two?
Just know I’ll be back for a sequel or cue!

Echoes of Untold Stories

In the attic of memories, tales untold,
Lurk ghosts of the past, both brash and bold.
They trip on the stairs, laugh quietly soft,
Whispering secrets, all joyfully scoffed.

With mismatched socks and a collection of memes,
My life was a sitcom, or so it seems.
Each page has its quirks, both wild and tame,
Who knew such nonsense could be my claim to fame?

As we gather these stories, mayhem unfolds,
Giggling at mishaps, and plans that were bold.
Remember the pie that hit me in the face?
How we screamed with laughter, lost in the space!

So here's to the echoes that fade yet remain,
A chorus of giggles, a sweet playful strain.
Though the curtain may fall on this loud, silly spree,
Every chuckle shall linger—remember, that's me!

A Tale Concluded

Once upon a time, or so they say,
A plot so twisted, it lost its way.
Characters danced, then tripped on a shoe,
In a story that ended, just ask the zoo.

The hero's saga came to a halt,
He forgot his sword, then slipped on a malt.
Villains sighed, all their plans fell flat,
As laughter erupted, they laughed as a cat.

The princess unwrapped her last piece of pie,
Declared it was time for a final goodbye.
She called all the knights for a witty roast,
As they served up tales, toast after toast.

And so it concludes, with a pie in the face,
A tale of mischief, not bound by grace.
Where endings are funny, not sad or bleak,
We wave to the readers, so come take a peek!

Shadows of Yesterday

In a world where shadows used to play,
Yesterday's laughter has drifted away.
With jokes in the margins, and giggles in ink,
The past wrote a script that's hard not to think.

The heroes, they trotted, with capes made of cheese,
Told tales of bravado while stuck in the breeze.
Granny threw cookies to run off the spies,
And everyone wondered just who wore the pies.

The dragon loved karaoke, oh what a sight,
Singing opera at dawn, to everyone's fright.
But once the sun set, he slept like a rock,
Dreaming of heroes who knocked and then knocked.

So shadows may linger, but laughter will stay,
While echoes of yesterday tickle the way.
We'll remember their antics and outlandish quests,
As we turn yet another page, laughing at best!

The Closing Lines

With pens dipped in giggles, we scribble our fate,
The plot twists and turns like a twisty old gate.
Characters argue over who gets the cheese,
As the chapter wraps up, they declare, "More please!"

A writer scratched his head, then sighed with a frown,
How do I finish this silly old clown?
The meaning of life? Just eat lots of cake,
And laugh with your friends for your own silly sake.

As pages turn yellow, and spines start to crack,
The hero insists, "We're never looking back!"
With belly laughs booming, they trudge to the core,
Where lessons are silly, but might leave you sore.

With a wink and a nod, we bid them adieu,
Their story, though nuts, was made just for you.
So close up the book with a grin ear to ear,
These closing lines echo with playful cheer!

Epilogue of Dreams

In the land of lost socks, where dreams often roam,
A troupe of old slippers formed a bright dome.
They gathered for tales, with popcorn in tow,
To share in the laughter, and silly old flow.

The clocks all chimed midnight, or was it a cat?
With fish bowls for thrones, they laughed where they sat.
The queen of the slippers declared it was time,
To end this grand saga, all silly but prime.

But dreams don't forget, they twist in the night,
With dragons and cupcakes all taking flight.
As stories collide with bubbly delight,
Who knew endings could just take off in flight?

So here's to the laughter, the fun never stops,
Where dreams will weave tales with flips and with hops.
As the epilogue closes, just know it's a tease,
A wink from the slippers, with giggles and ease!

Closing the Book

With ink still wet, my fingers fumble,
As I drop the pen and let out a grumble.
Characters gasp, plot twists in shock,
But here I am, closing the lock.

Once a hero, now a tired scribe,
Fading scenes with a shaky vibe.
The villain trips on his own cape,
Oh, that’s the end? What a great escape!

Silenced Sorrows

In the fridge, I find old leftovers,
Each bite whispers of forgotten endeavors.
The laughter fades, but here comes a pun,
Isn't that just the way life’s run?

Books stacked high, tales left untold,
Pages that crinkle, just like old gold.
Yet I chuckle, with a wink and wink,
Who knew endings could make one think?

Threads of Time

Time's woven tapestry, a messy thread,
I flip the fabric; oh look, that's Fred!
He never did make the big score,
Yet he stumbled in—what's one chapter more?

Bizarre plots dance, a comical spin,
As clocks tick on with a cheeky grin.
Lost in the folds of what we believe,
Threads unravel, but hey, let's not grieve!

A Journey's Last Farewell

So here we stand at this grand finale,
The shouting crowds and the confetti rally.
I check my notes; did I miss a line?
Oh well, let’s toast with soda and wine!

The hero waves, gives a silly pout,
While sidekicks argue about the route.
With laughter and giggles, we bid adieu,
In the end, it’s all a big déjà vu!

The Last Light Fades

The lights dim slow, all jokes aside,
Even the cats curl up to hide.
I comb through memories, the slip and slide,
Where laughter echoes, but now it's fried.

The curtain drops, applause is rare,
A rubber chicken strums the air.
I search for meaning, can't find a pair,
But hey, at least I can still wear flair.

Time waddles by, a silly dance,
My last big laugh? Oh, a missed chance!
The world spins on, a goofy prance,
Retired jokes, lost in a trance.

With giggles tucked, the end draws nigh,
A pie in the face? Oh me, oh my!
As shadows stretch and birdies fly,
I tip my hat to the goofy sky.

Reflections on the Edge

Standing tall on a wobbly chair,
I ponder life, and my lack of flair.
With mirrors cracking, can I even care?
Laughing at myself, it's a crooked affair.

The clock ticks loud, like a failed drum,
I dance a jig, though my legs feel numb.
Reflections wink, as if they're from mum,
Life's a mad caper, so here I come!

Jokes at hand, like candy in a jar,
I rummage through, beneath a fallen star.
The edge is near, but life's bizarre,
With silliness soaring, I'll raise the bar!

Adventure waits, with pie in the face,
Tickle the edge, in a wild embrace.
With laughter trailing, I'll run this race,
Until the last giggle, I'll keep up the pace.

Through the Haze of Time

Time floats by like a balloon in air,
With silly selfies and wild hair.
I squint through haze, a jester's glare,
Waving goodbye, but do I care?

Balloons and cakes, a circus parade,
The clowns are laughing, life’s a charade.
I juggle thoughts, in a fun escapade,
But the punchline's lost, let’s not be dismayed.

Through mists of moments, I trip and tumble,
While raindrops giggle, they make me fumble.
The clock’s hand spins, and I feel a rumble,
Each tick a joke, oh what a jumble!

Here’s to the chaos, the muddled time,
With a wink and a grin, oh isn’t it prime?
The dance floor’s waiting for my next rhyme,
So pop that balloon, let’s make it sublime!

The Darkening Horizon

The horizon blushes, a silly sight,
As pom-poms flair, it's happy hour light.
I squint and giggle, what a delight,
Jokes fading fast, but I won't take flight.

A pizza slice flies, oh watch it soar,
With cheese on my face, I fall to the floor.
Life's a comedy, just one big chore,
Yet laughter's the pay, who could ask for more?

Waves crash hard, with a giggly splash,
I ride on fun, I'm good at the bash.
As shadows wiggle, I won't be brash,
In this final jest, I'll make a mad dash!

But look at the stars, twinkling with glee,
A curtain call's near, come laugh with me.
With a wink to the night, let's all agree,
Even in darkness, we can still be free.

Final Breath of Words

In the book of life, I misplace a page,
The dog ate my homework, it's all the rage.
A pencil that giggles, a paper that flirts,
I write my regrets in invisible skirts.

The ink runs away, it knows I'm a fool,
Rubbing out stories like it's a school.
I laugh at my fate with a cup full of tea,
Living my life like an old melody.

So flip through the pages, my dear little friend,
Each line is a joke, where even cats bend.
In the margins are notes, they whisper, they sing,
As I dance into chaos, like a lost rubber ring.

And when the last sentence is finally drawn,
I'll pen it in sparkle, while wearing a fawn.
With a wink to the world, I'll tip my last hat,
And laugh at the ending, like a wise old cat.

Closure in Stillness

A sigh escapes from a dusty old tome,
Where the characters laugh, though they're miles from home.
Chapter closed with a twinge of delight,
As the cat on the cover begins to take flight.

What's that? A plot twist? Oh wait, it's a nap,
Falling through pages, oh what a mishap!
The plot thickens like gravy on fries,
As my tea spills over, to my great surprise.

I'll tip over tables of what could have been,
As my coffee gets cold, but I still can't win.
Slippers are dancing with glee on my feet,
As I doodle a story that's slightly offbeat.

The final punctuation? Oh, what is it now?
A smile, a chuckle, here's my best bow!
With laughter as echoes of stories long told,
I'll close up the book, but never the fold.

Written in Twilight

In a sunset giggle, my stories run wild,
The paper is sticky; it's laughter compiled.
Words tumble and twirl like a sweeper in glee,
As they trip over shadows and dance by the trees.

Twilight is sneaky, it plays hide and seek,
While my pen writes the secrets of every cheek.
I scribble in circles, then switch to a square,
Each line is a whisper that floats in the air.

For as night gently slips in, I'm caught in a dream,
With characters bursting like bubbles of cream.
The moon is my critic, all wise and so bright,
While I laugh at my sketches, oh what a sight!

When the last page is turned and the twilight does flee,
I'll sign off in stars; come and dance here with me!
With a wink and a twist, my tales become lore,
Written in twilight, who could ask for more?

Fragments of the Past

In a box of lost letters, where time likes to nap,
Old jokes are tucked neatly, in a delicate flap.
I find my high school crush, wrapped in a dream,
Where laughter-like candy spills out of the seam.

Photos in sepia, where my hair was a bird,
Flapping around like it never has heard,
I smile at the memories, tangled and spry,
As if time was a kite that forgot how to fly.

Each fragment I gather is silly and sweet,
Chronicles made of both blunders and heat.
I wear my past like a jester's fine crown,
For laughter is light, that can never weigh down.

So raise up your glasses to moments gone by,
With chuckles and sighs and a wink of the eye.
Though pages may yellow and stories may twist,
I savor each fragment—for they all still exist!

A Soft Farewell

When the curtain drops with a flop,
And the laughs just won't stop,
We dance like fools, one last show,
With silly hats and a bow.

A pie in the face, what a sight,
As we bid each other goodnight,
In this slapstick tale we weave,
Who knew it'd be hard to leave?

Jokes flying like confetti in air,
We reminisce over snacks we share,
With giggles muted, still we grin,
This light-hearted tale now wears thin.

So raise a glass of fizzy cheer,
To friendship and fun year after year,
As the final joke brings a tear,
We'll always find laughter here!

Coda in the Stillness

In the quiet, the giggles hang,
Like echoes of joy from when we sang,
The clock chimes, the hour is ripe,
For one last zany, silly type.

The grand finale, a pratfall galore,
With pies and puns, we can't ignore,
Then there's a slip, and down we go,
Belly laughs help soothe the blow.

We share a wink and a poke at fate,
As the ending fades, it feels so great,
In jest we tell the stories grand,
Of shenanigans that always were planned.

With every chuckle, we breathe a sigh,
As the silly moments flutter by,
A toast to the humor that always will be,
In this silly coda, so carefree!

The Last Light of Dawn

As morning breaks with a coffee spill,
We giggle at yesterday's wild thrill,
Time to pack our laughs in a box,
While racing cats and clumsy oxs.

The sun peeks in, a wink and a tease,
Promising chaos like a gentle breeze,
We frolic away, but not with gloom,
With a bounce in our step, we fill the room.

Slippers on and a dance in the hall,
We trip over laughter, we stumble and fall,
Yet in our hearts, the joy we share,
Makes this good-bye feel quite rare.

So here’s to the pranks and goofy delight,
In this bright dawn, we take flight,
With one last laugh, we vow to stay,
In silly memories, we’ll never stray!

Where Words Cease to Be

In the silence, we chuckle with glee,
As words fizzle out like a spent jubilee,
With nods and winks, we communicate,
In this giggle fest, we celebrate.

The final scene’s a hat made of cheese,
With rubber chickens that never seem to freeze,
Our script's a jumble, a playful feat,
Where punchlines are quickly on repeat.

We gather our thoughts, but they scatter wide,
Like candy at a parade we cannot hide,
In this crazy rush, our hearts take flight,
As humor weaves through the fading light.

So raise a glass to the laughter we spun,
In this whimsical journey, we’ve had our fun,
As words take a backseat, smiles take a seat,
In this end, our joy feels complete!

Threads of Farewell

In the book of life, we close with a grin,
Laughing at fates and the chaos within.
Characters tripping on words they can't spell,
Signing off early, oh what the hell!

Plot twists are wild, like cats on a spree,
Chasing their tails and deciding to flee.
We're heroes and villains, both jester and sage,
Dancing through chapters, let's set up the stage!

With coffee-spilled pages, we giggle and sigh,
Turning the covers, oh my, oh my!
Last line is here, but the fun will not end,
So grab your quill, let's all just pretend!

A wave of the pen, and a wink from the muse,
Ink stains on fingers, nothing left to lose.
We'll pen our next tale, with laughter resound,
In the library of life, joy does abound!

Twilight of the Written Word

As the ink runs dry, let’s twist it with flair,
A comical ending, let’s breathe in the air.
Characters waving, with a wink and a nod,
Kicking dust up and saying, 'Oh, that was odd!'

The pages are flipping, a whirlwind of fun,
Monsters in pajamas, they’re on the run.
Plot lines unravel like socks in the wash,
We giggle at chaos, just give it a squash!

In a world where the puns take center stage,
Life’s a big joke, we’ll all engage.
Letters and laughter dance in the breeze,
Ending our tale with a laugh and a tease.

So here’s to the close of this whimsical ride,
Let’s raise a glass to the joy that we tried.
The ink may be fading, but spirits are bright,
With chuckles and cheers, we bid you goodnight!

Beyond the Last Page

A parchment awaits, but the plot goes astray,
Characters plotting their cheeky getaway.
Pens tapping wildly like feisty little crabs,
Chasing their tales, avoiding the jabs.

With each silly scribble, we chuckle and cheer,
A hero's farewell with a slice of good beer.
The words dance and flutter, a joyous parade,
In this laugh-out-loud story we've cleverly made.

Closing the book but not closing the fun,
We're raising a ruckus; the adventure's begun!
Jokes in the margins, they wink and they tease,
Let's swipe our last line with a laugh and a breeze!

So here's our salute, to the tales that we tell,
With humor and heart, we've cast our own spell.
We'll scribble forever in joy, never rage,
For stories keep living, beyond every page!

Silence Between the Lines

In the quiet of pages where stories unfold,
Lively cheeky antics, both daring and bold.
Gaps filled with giggles, a chuckle or two,
As we nudge the last line, and bid it adieu.

The characters whisper, like secrets in air,
Witty as jesters, with humor to spare.
With puns worth their weight, they prance in a line,
Delivering laughter in rhythm and rhyme.

As we close up the cover, let's pop open cheer,
For the end is but laughter, let's keep it near.
We'll pen our new tale, with mischief in tow,
In the silence of lines, let the fun always flow.

So gather your quills; let's scribble a scene,
Where endings are funny and all in between.
The stories may pause, but the smiles will last,
With humor in hand, here's to future and past!

The End of the Road

The car broke down, what a sight,
We waved goodbye, with all our might.
We brought a map, but lost the lane,
In this comedy of errors, who’s to blame?

The GPS said, 'Turn left, oh please!'
We turned right into a swarm of bees.
With laughter loud, we danced and spun,
Guess this road trip is nowhere done!

The last gas station, a smelly old shack,
We filled the tank, then turned back.
With snacks galore, all crunched and fried,
We ended up with crumbs inside!

So here we sit, in the setting sun,
We’ll tell the tales of our silly run.
The end of the road? Just a brand new start,
For every end is a funny part!

Final Strokes of Memory

With brush in hand, I painted wide,
A sky of purple, and a green slide.
But every stroke brought giggles loud,
As I accidentally painted a cow-shaped cloud!

The canvas dry, I called my friend,
'What do you think? Is this the end?'
She laughed so hard, she spilled her tea,
'Your masterpiece is a sight to see!'

The final strokes, a twist of fate,
A mustache here, a goofy gait.
With every addition, the colors bled,
I now had a self-portrait of my cat instead!

So we display it on the wall with glee,
Art's all in fun, for you and me.
Memory frozen in strokes so bold,
Funny stories that never grow old!

The Last Breath of Ink

My pen ran dry, just like my luck,
Each word I wrote, a big ol' cluck.
I stamped my feet, I pulled my hair,
'Just write the end, but give me flair!'

One final line, I scratched my chin,
With thoughts of donuts and my next win.
Instead of wisdom, a doodle arose,
A cat in a hat, striking a pose!

The paper sighed, my ink ran out,
I'll tell you now, without a doubt.
In the realm of stories, some get a boon,
While others just end with a silly tune!

Yet still I smile, my page a mess,
With jumbled words, I couldn't stress.
For in this game of wit and fun,
The last breath of ink has just begun!

When Time Calls It Quits

Tick-tock goes the fateful clock,
Time waves goodbye, but with a mock.
To-do lists blow away in the breeze,
As I lounge around, doing as I please!

The hour hand trips, oh what a scene,
While moments slip by in a silly routine.
I lose track of days, just float about,
Laughing at clocks that try to shout!

When time calls it quits, we all cheer loud,
For naps and snacks beneath a cloud.
Chasing hours? That's quite the sport,
Instead, I'll nap, a perfect retort!

So raise a glass, to forgotten beats,
To playful times and funny feats.
When time bids adieu and fades from view,
We'll find joy in the silly things we do!

Last Notes of Mirth

When I declared I’d quit my jobs,
The cake was made of hairy mobs.
A party thrown, with laugh and cheer,
For all the things that brought us near.

I stumbled on a banana peel,
And cried, 'This was my last big deal!'
The life we led, so full of glee,
Who knew it ended with a spree?

I waved goodbye to my old desk,
Left behind my tasks grotesque.
They promised me a golden clock,
But gave me cake that smelled like stock.

So here’s to all the silly days,
Where laughter drove the mundane ways.
As I depart, I wear a grin,
And toss confetti on my skin.

The Unsaid Goodbye

I packed my bags with socks and ties,
Left all my woes and awkward sighs.
The door slammed shut, my heart did race,
I tripped on crumbs, my fall of grace.

The boss exclaimed, 'We'll miss your jokes!'
But only I knew I'd prank the blokes.
With jelly in the stapler, how fun!
Who'd ever think I'd outrun the sun?

It's time for laughs in a new place,
Where no one knows my quirks or grace.
I'll nod to ghosts who haunt my past,
And make them giggle, a spell so cast.

So raise a glass to messy times,
And flip the script with silly rhymes.
As I drift off without a care,
Remember, laughter's always there.

In the Wake of Silence

In quiet spots where echoes dwell,
I pondered deeply—what the hell?
The office chair creaked a tired tune,
While coffee brewed at half-past noon.

A mime came by to bid farewell,
His gestures grand, yet hard to tell.
I laughed out loud, then felt a kick,
I'd spilled my drink; oh, what a trick!

With silence looming, fun began,
I danced alone, a goofy man.
The mice in the walls, they joined with glee,
As I foxtrotted quite recklessly.

In this stillness, laughter reigns,
For joy's a gift that still remains.
So here's to jokes that will not fade,
And echoes of the fun we made.

Conclusively Yours

So here I sit, with final notes,
Doodling jokes on paper boats.
A fitting end, or just a jest?
I’ll say farewell with all my zest.

They told me that the fun would cease,
But I bequeath my humor's fleece.
With puns and laughs, oh what a twist!
Do miss me dearly, put me on your list!

My desk’s now fresh, a vacant sea,
But hopes and giggles sail with me.
For as this journey finds its close,
Just know, life’s meant for chuckles, oh those prose.

So here’s my take, I’ll sign my name,
A funny ending, a silly game.
With smiles and winks, I’m off I go,
In laughter, love, and fun’s warm glow.

Echoes of Closure

In a world where socks go to hide,
I found my plot twist underneath the tide.
Characters lost in a laughable chase,
Seeking the end in a snail's slow race.

Pants on their heads, they dance on the floor,
Chasing their tails, they're asking for more.
A chapter might end, but take a good look,
There's always a sequel in life's funny book.

Dramatic exits and backflips galore,
They trip on their laces and tumble for sure.
Each flip of the page, a giggle it brings,
With twists like balloon animals, life truly swings.

So here's to the antics, the quirks and the quips,
As we close up our stories with playful little flips.
Let laughter echo as we bid adieu,
For every ending, there's laughter anew.

The Last Page Turned

With bookmarks misplaced, we search for the end,
But oh, look! It's a cliffhanger, our faithful friend.
Characters doled out in a heap by the fire,
Yarning old tales packed with comedic desire.

The villain slips on a banana peel,
His grand escape turns to a wobbly wheel.
Plot lines unravel like grandma's old yarn,
With giggles and snickers, life's never a darn.

As the credits roll, we hear the last joke,
The protagonist trips, jumps, and finally chokes.
But laughter fills air as we close the book tight,
Ready for more shenanigans tomorrow night.

So raise up your cups, let the cheers loudly ring,
For endings that leave us with joy that they bring.
Each chuckle a reminder of stories we earn,
In the realm of the written, the last page is turned.

Whispers of Closure

Here we stand at the brink, sipping cold tea,
Debating if sunset is worth a wee spree.
Time winks at us from the corner of fate,
While kicking a cat, who simply won't wait.

A knock on the door, who could that be?
An old friend, a villain, maybe a flea?
We're plotting our end with a cake made of sly,
Laughter erupts, as the cat starts to fly.

Life's riddled with hiccups, and so might this tale,
A fish in a tuxedo starts to regale.
With secrets to share and a laugh on the soul,
Every good goodbye can make laughter the goal.

So toast to the moments, the quirky and fun,
In laughter, we find how our stories are spun.
Whisper sweet nothings and shout out some cheer,
Each closure a page that we'll hold ever dear.

Endings Unwritten

In the land of absurd, where odd is the norm,
A tale unfolds that spins like a storm.
The cows grow wings; the frogs start to sing,
In this world of whimsy, oh, what joy they bring.

As chapters collapse with a comedic flare,
The heroes keep dancing without a care.
Each twist leaves us chuckling, oh what a sight,
In the book of goodbyes, we just might ignite.

The curtain draws near, but not without jest,
A juggler, a lion, they put on a quest.
The end is a laugh, a balloon in the air,
Unwritten adventures in moments we share.

So gather around for a laugh and a cheer,
For endings unwritten, they bring us more cheer.
With each shout of joy and silliness spun,
In life's silly story, the fun has begun.